S0-BRD-956

Little Bear

Little Bear

Written by Diane Namm

Illustrated by Lisa McCue

My First READER

children's press ®

A Division of Scholastic Inc.

New York Toronto London Auckland Sydney
Mexico City New Delhi Hong Kong
Danbury, Connecticut

Library of Congress Cataloging-in-Publication Data

Namm, Diane.
  Little Bear / written by Diane Namm ; illustrated by Lisa McCue.–
[1st American ed.].
        p. cm. – (My first reader)
Summary: When it comes to eating, Little Bear definitely prefers honey
to potatoes, peas, tomatoes, or cheese.
  ISBN 0-516-22931-1 (lib. bdg.)   0-516-24633-X (pbk.)
  [1. Food habits–Fiction. 2. Bears–Fiction. 3. Stories in rhyme.] I.
McCue, Lisa, ill. II. Title. III. Series.   OCT   7 2004
  PZ8.3.N27Li 2003
  [E]–dc21
                          2003003634

Text © 1990 Nancy Hall, Inc.
Illustrations © 1990 Lisa McCue
Published in 2003 by Children's Press
A Division of Scholastic Inc.

1 2 3 4 5 6 7 8 9 10 R 12 11 10 09 08 07 06 05 04 03

Note to Parents and Teachers

Once a reader can recognize and identify the 16 words
used to tell this story, he or she will be able to read successfully
the entire book. These 16 words are repeated throughout the story,
so that young readers will be able to easily recognize
the words and understand their meaning.

The 16 words used in this book are:

bear	please
cheese	potatoes
eat	some
honey	tomatoes
I	what
little	will
not	would
peas	you

Little Bear, Little Bear,
would you eat potatoes?

6

Little Bear, Little Bear,

would you eat some peas?

Little Bear, Little Bear,
would you eat tomatoes?

11

Little Bear, Little Bear,

would you eat some cheese?

14

I will not eat potatoes!

15

I will not eat some peas!

16

I will not eat tomatoes!

I will not eat some cheese!

Not potatoes?
Not some peas?

Not tomatoes?
Not some cheese?

What will you eat, Little Bear?

I will eat some honey,

please!

28

ABOUT THE AUTHOR

Diane Namm is the author of more than twenty-five books for children and young adults. Formerly an editor in New York, Namm freelances for a children's entertainment production company, writes, and lives with her husband and children in Malibu, California.

ABOUT THE ILLUSTRATOR

Lisa McCue has illustrated more than 100 children's books for many major publishers. Over the years, McCue's art has been selected on numerous occasions to be represented in The Original Art show, honoring the best in children's book illustrations. She lives with her husband and two sons in Maryland.

Writing on front page. 6/16

10-04

ER   Namm, Diane
         Little Bear.

GAYLORD RG